Basic Skills

# Grammar & Punctuation

*Glenne Hutchings*

Published in association with The Basic Skills Agency

Hodder Murray

A MEMBER OF THE HODDER HEADLINE GROUP

Orders: please contact Bookpoint Ltd, 130 Milton Park, Abingdon, Oxon 0X14 4SB. Telephone: (44)01235 827720, Fax: (44) 01235400454. Lines are open from 9.00–5.00, Monday to Saturday, with a 24 hour message answering service. You can also order through our website at www.hoddereducation.co.uk

*British Library Cataloguing in Publication Data*
A catalogue record for this title is available from The British Library

ISBN-13: 978 0 340 78258 3

First published 2001
Impression number 10 9 8 7 6 5
Year 2007



Hodder Headline's policy is to use papers that are natural, renewable and recyclable products and made from wood grown in sustainable forests. The logging and manufacturing processes are expected to conform to the enviromental regulations of the country of origin.

Cover photo from Corbis
Typeset by Dorchester Typesetting Group Ltd.
Printed in Great Britain for Hodder Murray, a member of Hodder Headline,
338 Euston Road, London NW1 3BH by Hobbs the Printers Ltd., Totton, Hampshire

# Contents

# Contents

# Introduction

This book will show students how to remember basic grammar and punctuation more easily. A multi-sensory approach is used throughout, so that all preferred learning styles are catered for.

Key Stage 3 students who still find grammar and punctuation difficult, may have been taught **what** to learn, but not in a way that they are able to easily access and retain the information.

People do not all learn in the same way:

- some prefer to use their visual senses
- some prefer to use their auditory senses
- some prefer to use their kinaesthetic senses.

Students who learn to use a combination of these methods give themselves a far greater chance of remembering what they have learned.

If students find one method of learning particularly helpful then they will naturally use that method as a preference. However, in order to reinforce the learning it is important that a combination of these learning styles is used.

As well as emphasising preferred learning styles, this book also requires the students to use a variety of intelligences.

Throughout the book there is the opportunity for the student to use both inter-personal and intra-personal intelligences, so there will be exercises where the student is asked to work independently, and some where co-operation with others is required.

Some worksheets require a linear, logical approach, yet others will ask for a much more open visual approach.

At the start of a new topic, or where new information is included during the topic, an information box is given, clearly stating the overview of what is to be learned. This will suit right-brained learners. The exercises are then broken down into short, manageable chunks, which will suit left-brained learners.

As the person over-seeing the student's work, make sure that stages are not left out. When required to read parts out loud for example, ensure that this is done and not 'skipped'. Once a multi-sensory approach is taken to be the norm, it becomes an integral part of learning.

This book is not simply grammar and punctuation. It is also about thinking and understanding. Once the understanding is present, the rest will follow.

# Overview of Chapters

## 1 Sentences

Chapter 1 explains how to use full stops at the end of sentences and how to use commas to create pauses and to separate items in a list. There is an introduction to the colon and semi-colon.

## 2 Capital letters

This chapter covers the use of the capital letter for the start of sentences and for names of people and places. Other uses of capital letters are introduced, such as titles and the personal 'I'.

## 3 Questions

Students are encouraged to ask questions to form the basis of a planning tool. Planning is taken further, continuing to use 'where, what, why, when, who, how' and introducing organisational maps. The exclamation mark is introduced.

## 4 Apostrophe

Chapter 4 covers the use of the apostrophe for both ownership and contractions. Students are shown how to identify who owns what in writing and to understand that the apostrophe represents missing letter(s) in words like doesn't, didn't and I'll.

## 5 Sentence structure

Students will be asked to investigate what a sentence is and how it can be made more interesting with the addition of adjectives and adverbs. Students will become familiar with the use of nouns, verbs, pronouns, adjectives and adverbs.

## 6 Conjunctions and prepositions

Chapter 6 shows how to join short sentences with a conjunction. The use of prepositions is explored, including using prepositions in order to give clear indications.

## 7 Sequence and order

This chapter looks at sequence and logical order. It includes the ordering of ideas, sentences and paragraphs. The use of organising with maps is encouraged.

## 8 Written speech

In this chapter, students will be shown how to represent speech in writing. The chapter starts with identifying direct speech with the aid of cartoons, and follows on with how to set this out in writing.

## 9 Tenses

Chapter 9 introduces tenses: past, present and future, and enables students to write without mixing up the tenses. Practise is also given in agreement between the verb and the noun.

## 10 Odds and ends

In this chapter students will be reminded of the common mistake of the double negative; how punctuation can completely alter the meaning of the written word; how to know when to use ‘I’ or ‘me’; how to use common abbreviations of words, and how to have fun whilst looking for errors.

# The full stop

A sentence makes sense. It starts with a capital letter. It ends with a full stop.

Imagine a world without full stops. You might know what you have written down, but other people would have trouble understanding it.

Full stops given meaning to your writing.

▶ **Say** this passage out loud. There are no full stops.

The room was stuffed with books of all shapes and sizes the largest books were covered in dust and hadn't been touched in years there seemed to be no order to where anything was placed on the shelves it was obviously time the town appointed a new librarian unfortunately the town council had run out of money and could not afford to pay any wages

**1** Add five full stops to make the passage make sense.
*After each full stop the first word of the next sentence must be a capital.*

▶ **Read** the passage again, this time pausing slightly at each full stop.

▶ **Listen** carefully as you read. The meaning now becomes clear.

# Getting started

Worksheet

## *Carrying on with stopping*

Below are three full stops.

1 **Draw** a line to where you think each one should go in the passage that follows.

•   •   •

It was the end of the school holidays Anne was not looking forward to the new school term Emily had always been in the same class as Anne but now things were going to be different

2 **Write** three sentences of your own *but leave out the full stops.*

________________________________________

________________________________________

________________________________________

________________________________________

________________________________________

________________________________________

________________________________________

________________________________________

________________________________________

3 Ask a friend to spot where the full stops should go. Did your friend get it right?

## Putting a stop on it

Mark had just seen a robbery and was giving his story to the police. Trying to get his story out quickly, he hardly paused for breath.

I saw them there were two, no, three of them running out of the shop the owner was running behind shouting at them to stop at least I think there were three the third one could have been the owner I'm not sure anyway they didn't stop they just kept on running the first man knocked over a lady and didn't even stop to say sorry my mum would kill me if I did that do you want to know anything else?

The policeman re-wrote Mark's statement using sentences so that the court would understand it.

1 **Write** the report below, so that what Mark said makes sense. Use a capital letter at the start of each sentence and a full stop at the end.

### Police Report

**Witness statement given by Mark Jones.**

__________________________________________________________

__________________________________________________________

__________________________________________________________

__________________________________________________________

__________________________________________________________

__________________________________________________________

__________________________________________________________

__________________________________________________________

__________________________________________________________

Signed.........................................

# Getting started

## *Commas*

If there is a list in a sentence, a comma is used to separate each item.

If the last two items in a list are joined by the word 'and' you do not usually need a comma as well unless it helps to make the meaning clearer.

**1** Add commas to the lists in these sentences:

**a** When planning my walking holiday I had to remember to pack a compass map spare pair of socks plasters and a raincoat.

**b** The cake recipe called for flour butter sugar and eggs.

**c** I left my work until the last minute and ended up having to do two essays for art and research for a project all on the same night.

▶ **Read** each sentence out loud, first without the commas, then with the commas. Which is easier to understand?

Below is a shopping list written on a scrap of paper.

bananas dog food washing up liquid cereal
pizza cheese butter

**2** Add a comma after each item to make the list easier to follow.

# Commas 2

Commas give a short pause in a sentence, making the meaning clearer.

Some sentences may become confusing if the commas are left out. For example:

*Mark the captain of the football team sprained his ankle and could not play.*

By adding commas we make the meaning clearer:

*Mark, the captain of the football team, sprained his ankle and could not play.*

▶ **Read** the sentences below out loud:

**a** Angela best friend of Susan wanted to go to watch the banger racing.

**b** Susan who had known Angela for a long time didn't want to go, as she wanted to see Tom instead.

**c** Tom who didn't like banger racing anyway said he was going to the football match.

**1** Now add two commas to each sentence to help make the meaning clearer.

▶ **Read** the sentences again, **listening** to the slight pause at each comma.

Worksheet 1 Getting started

## *Catch the comma!*

Five commas have escaped from this passage.

**1** Draw a line from each comma to where it should go.

, , , , ,

The long golden beach stretched out in front of her. The sea was a mixture of blues greens and flecks of gold. Three whole weeks to do nothing but swim sunbathe and laze around. Sally who had never been here before thought she was in heaven.

- **Ask** a partner to read the passage out loud to you now that you have added the commas.

Have you put the commas in the right place?

- **Discuss** this with your partner. Do you agree?
- **Check** your answers with your teacher.
- **Look** at the list of words below:

| *happy moody tall short blue-eyed* |
|---|
| *brown-eyed nervous thin giggly straight-haired* |
| *curly-haired intelligent friendly short-tempered mean* |

**2** Write one sentence to describe your partner, using at least three of the words above. Use commas where they are needed.

________________________________________

________________________________________

# *Semi-colon (;)*

| The semi-colon can be used to separate phrases in a list. |
|---|

In the worksheet on commas, we saw how using a comma separates words in a list.

Sometimes a semi-colon (;) can help as well. If the sentence has a list that includes phrases rather than single words, then the comma doesn't give a long enough pause. We use a semi-colon instead.

For example:

*The campers had remembered the kettle, for boiling water; the stove, for heating the kettle; sleeping bags, to keep them warm at night, and the tent.*

This is a list that Peter jotted down when he wanted to make a cake.

milk, for mixing
sugar, to cream with the butter
flour, to stir into the mixture
eggs to make it rise

**1** Write the list into a sentence, using semi-colons to separate the phrases.

To make his cake, Peter needed:

______________________________________________

______________________________________________

______________________________________________

______________________________________________

# Getting started

Worksheet

## Colon (:)

The colon introduces us to information that follows.

A colon may be used before a quotation, or a sign.

For example:

*Public Notice: Keep off the grass.*

A colon may be used to show who is saying what – such as in jokes, or plays.

For example:

*Boy: 'Why have African elephants got big ears?'*
*Girl: 'I don't know. Why have African elephants got big ears?'*
*Boy: 'Because Noddy won't pay the ransom.'*

A colon may be used to introduce a list.

For example:

*There are three kinds of horses: racing horses, cart horses and rocking horses.*

**1** Add colons to these examples:

Somerset County Council No ball games.

Woman 'Do you have broccoli?'
Shopkeeper 'No, Madam, it's just the way I'm standing.'

There are three kinds of money to have money, lots of money and lots more money.

# Colon 2

A colon may be used to add more information to a sentence.

**Look** at this sentence:

*There are two ways of solving this problem: the right way and the wrong way.*

The first part of the sentence introduces the topic, the second part adds more information. A colon is used between the two parts.

The following sentences may be divided into two parts by using a colon.

**Read** each sentence out loud. See if you can **hear** where the colon should come.

1 **Write** the colon into each sentence.

Don't blow out my candle it won't make yours burn any brighter.

Jane's exam results were good 3 'A's and 2 'B's.

Her clothes suited her personality dull and lifeless.

We came to an agreement about money what's mine is mine and what's his is mine.

Beware the light at the end of the tunnel the train coming in the opposite direction has bright headlights.

# Capital letters

## Capital letters

| A sentence always starts with a capital letter. |
|---|

1 In the following sentences:
**cross out** the small letter at the start of each sentence and **write** the capital letter above.

the boy fell over and hurt his knee.

our football team won the league last year.

school examinations start next week.

▶ **Look** at the picture.

Using a sentence, describe what the man is doing:

______________________________________________

______________________________________________

Make sure you put a capital letter at the start of the sentence.

## More sentences

The local newspaper reported on a new business idea but they had problems with their printing.

1 Go through the following report, putting in the capital letter at the start of each sentence.

### JOBS BOOST!

three local people have just agreed a deal that should bring hundreds of jobs to the area. this unusual scheme involves bottling small quantities of local soil and selling it as 'Real Country Memories'. customers will be able to choose smells such as 'Farmyard Chicken', 'Cow Delight' and 'Meadow Surprise'.

▶ **Look** carefully at the report again.

2 **Draw** a circle around the capital letter at the start of each sentence.

3 **Underline** any other capital letters in the report.
*Notice that the names of the products start with capital letters.*

4 In the space below **write** each capital letter that you have circled or underlined.

# Capital letters

Worksheet

## *Looking at the problem*

▶ **Look** carefully at the sentences below.

1 **Find** the mistakes at the start of the sentences.

▶ **Draw** a big circle around any mistakes.

Kate was a friendly girl. she liked to be kind to her friends and to animals. one of her favourite animals was her cat, Smokey. Smokey was small and black and he would follow Kate wherever she went. when it was time for his meal, Smokey would remind Kate by meowing loudly.

To help you remember to put a capital letter at the start of each sentence, use the **full stop** as a memory trigger.

| After a full stop the next sentence must start with a capital letter. |
|---|

2 In the next paragraph **colour** each full stop in a bright colour and also the capital letter that comes next:

Once, there were two brothers who lived quietly together in a cottage in the country. They went to the local school. One brother was a pupil and one a teacher. Peter never wanted to go to school in the mornings. He would stay in bed until the last minute, then he'd say he was too ill to go because he had a bad stomach or a pain in his leg. One day he even said that he had a fat eyelash which stopped him seeing properly. The big problem was that Peter was the headteacher.

## *Hearing when to do it*

**Listening** carefully can help you to decide where one sentence ends and the next begins.

- Ask someone to read the paragraph below **out loud** to you, pausing very slightly between sentences.
- Raise your hand each time one sentence finishes and the next begins.

The sea looked beautiful. Small waves rippled towards the shore, each one a whole range of blue and green. Sun shimmered on the top of each wave, sending little sparkles of light in all directions. Becky sighed. She longed to be swimming in that sea instead of just watching it on a television programme about holidays.

- Now read the passage **out loud** yourself, pausing at the end of each sentence to circle the next capital letter.

Carry on listening.

- **Read** the next passage out loud. All the full stops and capital letters have been left out.
- **Listen** carefully to where you think the sentences should start and finish.
- **Write** in the full stops and capital letters.

the supermarket manager was not happy he had wanted to sell more tins of cat food this week than any other shop the trouble was his customers said that their cats wouldn't eat it

# Capital letters

## *More listening*

Poems usually have capital letters at the start of each line.

▶ **Read this poem out loud.**

'Listen to me,' said the teacher.
'Work can always be fun.
Think of work as a pleasure
And it will quickly be done.'

'Oh no,' said the pupil with sadness,
'I'm afraid that's simply not right.
My homework is just not as interesting
As the upper school disco tonight.'

▶ Now **write it** below not as a poem but in ordinary sentences:
*(Remember to put a capital letter at the start of each sentence.)*

▶ **Leave out** capital letters that might have been used in the poem but aren't needed in ordinary sentences.

_______________________________________________

_______________________________________________

_______________________________________________

_______________________________________________

_______________________________________________

# Names

A **proper** noun always starts with a capital letter. A proper noun is a real name – of a person, place, or thing.

1 Write your own name below, making sure you start each name with a capital letter.

___

The list below is part of a class register.

The person who wrote it forgot to put in the capital letters.

2 Cross off the small letters that are wrong and write the capital above.

**Class 3Y**

amy aster

becky baxter

claire cuthbert

dale dean

emily ensor

frazer farmer

greg gardner

henry harvey

ian imber

# Capital letters



## *I am important*

When you use 'I' to refer to yourself, it is always a capital letter.

You are an important person. There is only one of you.

When you refer to yourself you say **I**.

Because you are important **I** is always a capital.

There is no other reason to have **I** on its own in writing, so if you see it standing around by itself, you know it should be a capital letter.

**I** am important.

1 **Write** this in the space, writing the 'I' in your own style and colour.

2 **Write** three sentences about yourself, all starting with 'I'.

1 ______________________________

2 ______________________________

3 ______________________________

3 Join two of the sentences together, using a conjunction (a joining word) – you might use *and, but, although,* or another word of your own choice.

______________________________

______________________________

# More names

We have already seen that capital letters are needed for *the beginning of a sentence, names of people*, and when you use *'I'* to refer to yourself.

Other words that need capitals are:

names of places
names of months
names of days
titles – for instance of books or people

**1** Complete this list for the months of the year:

January February __ __ __ __ __ April __ __ __ June
__ __ __ __ August September __ __ __ __ __ __ __
November __ __ __ __ __ __ __ __

**2** Look at the list of the days of the week below. Can you **see** what is wrong?

▶ Correct the mistakes in a bright colour.

Monday tuesday wednesday Thursday friday
Saturday sunday

If a person has a title at the front of their name, it always has a capital letter. For example, Dr Johnson, Mrs Smith.

**3** Write these names, using the correct title:

Your teacher ____________________

Your doctor ____________________

Your friend ____________________

# Capital letters



## *Using what you know*

**1** You have been paid a large sum of money to write an exciting book.

It can be about anything you want, but the opening paragraph has to have something to do with this picture and a man called Mr Jones.

The first sentence is written for you.

▶ **Write** the next sentences.

Mr Jones was no good with fireworks.

In fact he was so bad that ______________________________

______________________________________________

______________________________________________

______________________________________________

______________________________________________

______________________________________________

Have you put a **capital letter** at the **start** of each sentence and for **proper names**?

## Just checking

▶ **Look** for the real names in these sentences.

1 **Circle** each name.

2 **Write** the names out correctly below.

mark johnson was the leader of the local council. He was well known by everyone – or so they thought. mark started doing things that were quite unexpected. He would arrange to meet vicky weston and john smith who were both on the council and then just not turn up. sue marsh saw him waiting for someone in the car park but then he said he hadn't been there at all. His secretary, sandra wills, said he had started to be like two different people. All was made clear at the staff party when mark introduced his identical twin andrew, who loved to play tricks on people.

**Names:**

______________________ ______________________

______________________ ______________________

______________________ ______________________

## Asking questions

> If you ask a question, a question mark is needed at the end of the sentence.

This is a question:
*When is your birthday?*

This is a statement:
*He asked me when my birthday is.*

The question is asking for information. It expects an answer. A statement tells you something. It does not expect an answer.

- **Look** at the sentences below.
- **Say** each sentence out loud to check whether it is a question or a statement.

**1** Write a question mark at the end of the sentences that are questions.

**2** Write a full stop at the end of sentences that are not questions.

1 Would you like to go to the disco tonight

2 She asked if I would like to go to the disco tonight

3 She wanted to know how many sugars I had in my tea

4 How many sugars do you have in your tea

5 Are you going on holiday this year

6 I am going on holiday this year

## More questions?

Questions may often begin with: who, why, what, where, when.

*Who are you?*
*Why did you do that?*
*What do you want?*
*Where are you going?*
*When will you get there?*

**1** Write down five questions to ask a friend. Start each question with the word given.

▶ **Say** the words 'question mark' as you write **?** at the end of each question.

Who ________________________________

Why ________________________________

What ________________________________

Where ________________________________

When ________________________________

# Questions

## *Questions that find the answer*

*who, what, why, where, when*

You can use these words to find information from a piece of writing.

- **Read** the passage below.
- **Answer** the questions below.

Johnny found it hard to fit in at school. He was an unusual child. He was keen on music and World War II. He dug tunnels in the back yard like the soldiers in Vietnam. Then he went into the tunnel and waited for it to fall in on him.

When he was twelve Johnny's mum got him an electric guitar. He shut himself in his room and learned to play.

Johnny hated school. He was very bored. He got in with a bad crowd and started stealing and taking drugs. But all that stopped when he was fifteen.

*(Extract from Livewire Real Lives, Johnny Depp.)*

1 **Who** is this passage about?

___________________________________________

2 **What** did his mum buy Johnny when he was twelve?

___________________________________________

3 **Why** didn't Johnny fit in at school?

___________________________________________

4 **Where** did Johnny dig tunnels?

___________________________________________

5 **When** did Johnny stop stealing and taking drugs?

___________________________________________

# Questions that help us plan

If you are planning a holiday, there will be many questions that you will need to answer.

These might include:
**Where** do you want to go? By the sea or in the country?
**When** do you want to travel? By day or by night?
**How** do you want to travel? By car? By ship? By plane?
**Who** do you want to go with? Your family? Your friends?
**What** do you want to do when you get there? Lie on the beach? Visit museums? Spend all your time clubbing?

Instead of writing all this out in a long list, try mapping it:

Where? ________________

When? ________________

Who with? ________________

**Holiday**

What do I want to do? ________________

How to travel? ________________

*(You don't even have to use words – you could draw pictures.)*

# Questions



## *More mapping with questions*

You can use mapping with questions to help you plan your own writing.

If you are asked to do a piece of writing, it can be difficult to organise your thoughts.

Some people like to make lists.

Some people like to put ideas down on separate cards.

Some people like to map.

▶ **Look** at the map below.

This is how one pupil put down all her ideas for an essay she had been asked to write about her school.

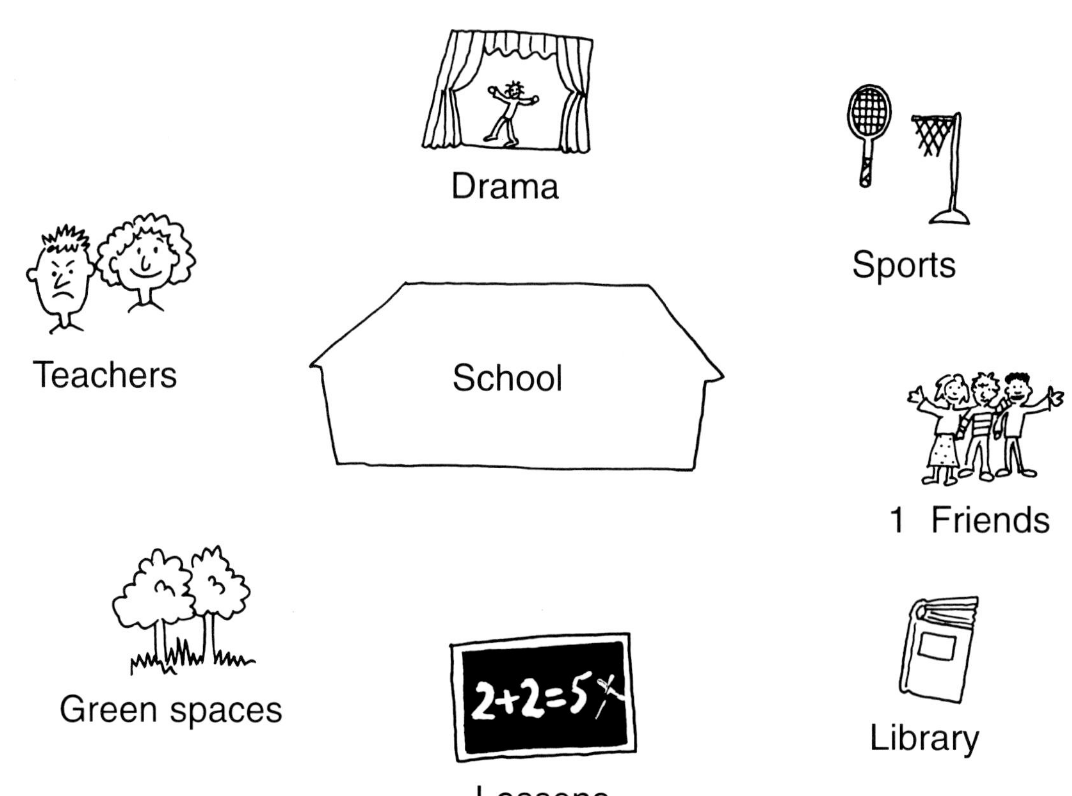


Number each point in the order you think each idea should be used. Number 1 has been filled in.

# Mapping for yourself

▶ **Choose** a subject that you would like to map.

It could be yourself, your school, a hobby, a book review or anything else you choose.

**1** Write the main subject in the middle of the page.

**2** Ask questions – who, what, where, when, why, how to help you put down the information you need.

**3** Draw pictures instead of writing words if you prefer.

▶ **Use** colours to make your ideas stand out.

▶ When you have finished, number each idea in the order that you would like to use it.

You have now organised your essay.

# Questions

## The exclamation mark

Want to make a strong statement? Use an exclamation mark!

Sometimes you may want to put more emphasis into what you say than a full stop will allow. Using an exclamation mark can make your words stronger.

You can use the exclamation mark to give a command:

*Put that down!*

*Get out of here!*

To call for help:

*Help! Help!*

*I'm stuck! Somebody help me!*

To show surprise or anger:

*This class had better get down to work or you'll all stay in after school!*

*I didn't expect you to hand this in so soon!*

- **Read** the next passage below out loud.
- **Read** it a second time and change full stops to exclamation marks where you think they would be better.

She looked awful. Her hair was long and straggly, and not only that, it was bright pink. Her clothes had to be seen to be believed. She was only fourteen, and went to the local school. Her teachers had turned a blind eye to her clothes so far, hoping that she would grow out of it. Looks like they'll have a long wait.

# The apostrophe (possession)

> To show that something belongs, use the apostrophe.

In the following sentences, **look** to see who owns what:

*The boy's book. (The book belonging to the boy.)*

*The teacher's desk. (The desk belonging to the teacher.)*

*The hen's food. (The food belonging to the hen.)*

*The hens' food. (The food belonging to the hens.)*

To show ownership, the apostrophe is used before the s. If there is more than one owner, as in the last example, the apostrophe is used after the s.

- **Look** at the examples that follow.
- **Say** each one out loud, then say who owns what.
  *(E.g.: The hen's food. The food belongs to the hen.)*

**1** Write down who the owner is, then what is owned.
*(E.g.: Owner: the hen. What is owned: the food.)*

1 The girl's skirt.
Owner: ____________ What is owned: ______________

2 The cat's milk.
Owner: ____________ What is owned: ______________

3 My brother's bike.
Owner: ____________ What is owned: ______________

4 My brothers' bikes.
Owner: ____________ What is owned: ______________

# Apostrophe



## More ownership

In the following passage, all the apostrophes that show who owns what, have been left out.

1 Draw a circle where each apostrophe has been left out.

2 Write in the missing apostrophe in a bright colour.

- For each apostrophe you write in, fill in the table below. The first one has been done for you.

David's timetable was not looking good. His mothers last words when he left home that morning were to remind him to work hard. His teachers comments on his last report showed that his work in all subjects needed to improve. This timetable was a nightmare. Uncle Jakes building firm was looking for workers. Should he forget about school and his mothers plans for him and become a wage earner? The countrys laws, however, had different ideas. It said that he had to stay at school until he was 16, and David was only seven.

| | **Owner** | **What is owned: =** | **+ apostrophe** |
|---|---|---|---|
| 1 | David | timetable | David's timetable |
| 2 | | | |
| 3 | | | |
| 4 | | | |
| 5 | | | |

## *Let's make it shorter*

**1** Read this passage out loud:

*It is* a cold and wet day. *Is not* it always the same when *you have* planned to do something outside? I *cannot* understand why the weather forecasters *are not* a little more correct. I *should have* brought my raincoat, but I *did not* think about it. Oh well, *it is* too late now. *I will* just have to get wet.

**2** Replace each word in italics with its shortened form. Write it out underneath. The words in the box will help you.

| | |
|---|---|
| didn't | isn't |
| it's | you've |
| I'll | can't |
| should've | aren't |

**3** Read the passage again in its shortened form.

# Apostrophe

Worksheet

## *Mixing them up*

This worksheet uses apostrophes both to shorten words and to show ownership.
All you have to do is sort out which is which!

**Remember** *it's = it is*

When you use *its* to show ownership (e.g.: The dog went into *its* kennel) you do not need an apostrophe.

1 **Read** the following passage.

Peter's house was cold and dark. Its windows were dirty and the next door neighbour's weeds poked through the broken fence. He knew he should've warned someone that he was coming, but it wouldn't do to tell people all your business would it? Besides which, Mrs Price's wages for looking after the house weren't small. She could've done a better job than this.

2 **Circle** three words that have been shortened with an apostrophe.

3 **Write** the full version out below:

______________________________

______________________________

______________________________

4 Find three things that are owned by somebody in the passage and write them below:

______________________________

______________________________

______________________________

# Sentences

A sentence must make sense.

Building a sentence is like building a wall. If you miss out one of the bricks, the wall will collapse.

If you miss out an essential part of a sentence, it will not make sense.

**1** Look at the sentences below. Read them out loud.
**2** Suggest a word that could be added somewhere in the sentence to make the words make sense.

1 James to the library. ____________________

2 The was shut. ____________________

3 My bus late. ____________________

4 What you want? ____________________

5 Emma ran towards the. ____________________

6 Last Christmas I had a for a present. ____________________

7 I hate doing. ____________________

8 I like sweets but I not like beans. ____________________

9 The insects were. ____________________

10 I know a. ____________________

# Sentences

Worksheet

## *Carrying on with sentences: nouns*

What is the recipe for success?

Every sentence must have a subject (usually a noun).
Every sentence must have a verb.
These are the two basic ingredients.

### *Nouns*

What is a noun?
A word that names anything is a noun.

There are different types of nouns. We will look at proper nouns and common nouns.

### Proper nouns

A proper noun begins with a capital letter.
The real name of something is a proper noun.
E.g.: Buckingham Palace, Mr Will Smith.

Your own name is a proper noun.

▶ **Write** your own name below.

______________________________

Each word in your name starts with a capital letter.

### Common nouns

A common noun names something that does not have a 'given' name.
E.g.: table, chair, desk, pen, pigsty, grass, tree, computer, glass.

A common noun does not have a capital letter.

▶ **Write** the name of three common nouns below:

______________

______________

______________

# Finding nouns

A proper noun is the real name of a person, place or thing.
It starts with a capital letter.

A common noun names something e.g.: table, chair.

- **Look** carefully at the words below.
- **Write** C next to each common noun.
- **Write** P next to each proper noun.

pencil _______ paper _______ The Eiffel Tower _______

computer _______ New York _______ England _______

Manchester United _______ London _______

island _______ treasure _______ grass _______

curtain _______ bed _______

# Sentences

## *Proper nouns and common nouns*

No more clues.

On the last worksheet, if you chose which were proper nouns and which were common nouns because one started with a capital letter, the next exercise will make you think again!

- **Write** each word again. Use a capital letter to start proper nouns.
- **Draw** a line to show whether the word is a proper noun or a common noun.

*(the first two have been done for you.)*

**proper noun** | **common noun**

BRISTOL Bristol | RIVER river

BOOK _______ PEN _____

SCHOOL _________ RIVER AVON ______________

CORONATION STREET __________________________

GIRL _____ TEACHER ______________

MRS JONES ______________

CHURCH ____________ TELEPHONE ______________

# Hunt the noun

- **Read** the following passage out loud.
- **Underline** each common noun in one colour.
- **Underline** each proper noun in another colour.

The waste-bin overflowed with rubbish. All the younger pupils had eaten their crisps and thrown the packets in the tiny bins which just weren't big enough. To make matters worse, each night the squirrels came and emptied the bins as they looked for food. Mrs Jones, the school caretaker, was getting fed up. No sooner had she cleaned up than the place was full of rubbish again. The school was called 'Brightmore'. Mrs Jones thought that it should be called 'Rubbishmore'. She was not happy. When she agreed to become caretaker she thought that she would be dealing with heaters and school repairs, not chocolate wrappers and half-eaten sandwiches.

How many did you find?

- **List** the common nouns in column A and the proper nouns in column B.

| A | B |
|---|---|
| ____________________ | ____________________ |
| ____________________ | ____________________ |
| ____________________ | ____________________ |
| ____________________ | ____________________ |
| ____________________ | ____________________ |

# Sentences

Worksheet

## *Nouns - use your own*

▶ **Use** these nouns in five sentences of your own.

You may use as many as you like in each sentence.

| | | | |
|---|---|---|---|
| palace | king | throne | King George |
| street | royal | flower | gold |
| paper | pencil | Mr Smith | exam |
| birthday | card | stamp | horse |
| saddle | rider | computer | keyboard |
| letters | telephone | address | number |
| stamp | | | |

These three sentences are started for you. You do not have to use them if you don't want to.

1 In the palace ______________________________

2 The rider put the saddle on ______________________________

3 The birthday card ______________________________

1 ______________________________

______________________________

2 ______________________________

______________________________

3 ______________________________

______________________________

4 ______________________________

______________________________

5 ______________________________

# The second Ingredient: the verb

A verb tells us what something, or someone, does.

A sentence can be as short as two words, as long as you have a subject (usually a noun) and a *verb*.

Dogs *bark*. Fish *swim.* Ships *float.*

▶ **Fill in** the missing verbs:

Birds _________. Perfume _________. I _________.

A sentence can be much longer, but still must have a **subject** (usually a noun) and a *verb*.

The **boy** *walked* along the dark, cold street.

**Asha** *hated* her new blue school jumper.

▶ **Fill in** the missing verb:

David __________ towards the main entrance.

After school Andrew __________ home.

Rebecca __________ when her cat died.

The library shelves __________ under the weight of all the heavy books.

The leaves _________ on the tree, the flowers _________ in the garden and my eyelids __________ heavy.

## Doing more with verbs

**1** Circle the verbs in this passage:

Mark ran quickly towards the edge of the forest. He saw a bright light deep in the undergrowth. Quietly and carefully he crept towards the light. A twig broke under his foot. He ran away.

You should have five circles.

**Check** that each circle is around a word that tells you what somebody or something did.

In this list, some of the words are verbs (doing words) and some are nouns (naming words).

**2** Circle the verbs.

**3** Underline the nouns.

| | | | | |
|---|---|---|---|---|
| tree | run | sing | telephone | card |
| hit | read | book | turn | sit |
| paper | news | pen | Mr Smith | push |

**4** Fill in the missing verbs below. You may use any that will make the sentence make sense.

1 I _________ the ball as hard as I could.

2 He _________ towards me at great speed.

3 I _________ in the cold water for half an hour.

# Pronouns

You can use a pronoun to replace a noun.

Instead of using somebody or something's name, you can replace it with a pronoun.

For example: *Peter's wife was strange.*
*Becomes:* ***His*** *wife was strange.*

▶ **Look** at the following list of pronouns:

| he | her | she | I | my |
|---|---|---|---|---|
| we | our | your | their | me |
| his | mine | you | they | |

**1** With a partner, take turns in choosing a suitable pronoun to fill in the gaps below. *(You do not have to write them down.)*

1 _________ luggage went missing.

2 _________ did not have her pen.

3 Is this _________ sister?

4 It belongs to me. Put it down it's _______

5 Is _________ throat sore?

6 _________ could not find his football boots.

7 The whole team had lost _________ football boots. _________ could not be found anywhere.

# Sentences

Worksheet

Basic Skills: Grammar and Punctuation

## *Adverbs*

An adverb describes *how* you do something.

*Jack sang.*

*Jack* is the noun. *Sang* is the verb. These are our two main ingredients in a sentence.

If we want to know **how** Jack sang, we use an adverb:
Jack sang *loudly. Loudly* is the adverb.

**1** Carry out the following instructions in the way the adverb tells you to.

1 Pick up your pen *slowly.*

2 Stand up *quickly.*

3 Raise your right hand *suddenly.*

4 Sit down *carefully.*

**2** With a partner give each other the instructions above, but this time change the adverb.

You might use:

| | | | |
|---|---|---|---|
| clumsily | loudly | vertically | clearly |
| horribly | awkwardly | completely | |
| happily | terribly | badly | |

# Adjectives

| Adjectives *describe* something. |
|---|

Adjectives are our next ingredient in making an interesting sentence.

| excellent | brilliant | marvellous | horrible | hateful |
|---|---|---|---|---|
| large | short | dull | bright | red |
| green | beautiful | ugly | | |

These are all examples of adjectives. There are lots more.

**1** Look around the room.

▶ **Choose** one person to describe. (Don't tell anyone who it is.)

**2** Fill in the following sentences using adjectives to describe this person.

This person has __________ hair that is also __________.

This person is __________.

This person is wearing __________ shoes and __________ trousers (or skirt).

This person __________ sometimes.

▶ **Ask** a partner to guess who you are describing.

# Sentences



## *More describing*

Colours are adjectives.

▶ **Close** your eyes and imagine something in the following colours. (Look up and to the left to remember a visual image.) (Look to the right if you are left handed.)

1 **Write** down what you see:

A red ______________

An orange ___________

A deep blue __________

Green ______________

Dark brown __________

2 **Describe** this person.

# *Making the most of adjectives*

Adjectives bring your writing alive.

Using *nice* to describe something tells us very little about it. Yet *nice* is one of the most over-used adjectives.
There are many ways to describe something.

▶ **Replace** *nice* in these descriptions with something more interesting:

1 It was a nice party.

______________________________

______________________________

2 They were nice people.

______________________________

______________________________

3 The food was nice.

______________________________

______________________________

4 The presents were nice.

______________________________

______________________________

You might want to use some of these words to help you:

delightful brilliant interesting delicious
exciting wonderful enchanting.

# 6 Conjunctions

## Conjunctions

Conjunctions are used to join short sentences together.

The following words: *although, after, and, as, because, before, but, if, of, unless, until, when, where, while* – are all examples of words that may be used as conjunctions.

- **Read** the sentences below out loud.
- **Underline** a conjunction in the list above to join the two sentences together.
- **Say** your new sentence.
- **Write** it out.

1 Sam and Jim went to the library. It was closed.

______________________________________________

______________________________________________

2 I have missed the bus. I will have to wait for the next one.

______________________________________________

______________________________________________

3 I don't like cabbage. I was made to eat it when I was little.

______________________________________________

______________________________________________

4 He was found innocent of the charges. Some people still thought he was guilty.

______________________________________________

______________________________________________

# Carrying on with conjunctions

The following sentences have not been finished.

- **Read** each sentence out loud, finishing it in an unusual way.
- **Share** your idea with a friend.
- **Decide** whose ending you like best.

*(You do not have to write your answers down.)*

1 I hate my job because ______________________________

2 I love my job but ______________________________

3 I will go on holiday unless ______________________________

4 Sam and John were best friends until______________________________

5 Ian said he'd do the washing up although ______________________________

6 Close the door before ______________________________

- Finish the words below to make examples of conjunctions.

b __________ s __________ wh __________ i__________

be ______________ un ______________

a ______________ af ______________ bef ______________

# Conjunctions

## *More conjunctions*

▶ Add the right word from the box to complete the sentences.

The first one is done for you.

| but | because | so | because | until | unless |
|---|---|---|---|---|---|

1 Tony and I will go to town but we must not miss the last bus home.

2 We lost the netball match ____________ our shooter broke her leg.

3 I lost the keys to my house ____________ I asked the policeman to help me get in.

4 I wanted a cup of tea ____________ I was thirsty.

5 We had to wait outside ____________ the owner came to open up the shop.

6 We will have to walk ______________ you give us a lift.

▶ **Read** each finished sentence out loud to check that it makes sense.

> A preposition shows us where something is in relation to something else.

| across | through | back | front | on | in | under | over | up | down |
|---|---|---|---|---|---|---|---|---|---|

The words in the box are all examples of prepositions. For example:

*The dog was* ***in*** *his bed.*

The word *in* tells us where the dog was in relation to his bed. He was *in* his bed.

**1** Find your way around this paragraph by writing in the missing prepositions.

The hen hopped ____________ from its perch straight ________ top of the waiting cat. The cat, taken by surprise, leaped _________ the hen house, out of the door and __________ the garden table. The hen didn't seem to notice. She walked ____________ the open door towards the __________ of the house; hopped __________ the half door of the kitchen and ate the cat's breakfast.

Worksheet

# Prepositions: Say it like it is

**1** Fill in the missing prepositions.

**2** Draw a picture to go with each sentence.

1

The cat is _______ the table.

2

The dog is _________ his bed.

3

The car drove _________ the bridge.

4

She went _________ the road.

**3** Underline the prepositions in the following paragraph.

The boy walked into the school. He was not happy. He had left his homework on the kitchen table and the cat had sat on it. When the cat sat on it she was wet. Now his homework was wet.

# Getting harder: Conjunctions and prepositions together

This page may be called 'Getting harder' but really it's having some fun.

The following sentences need to be joined by a conjunction (a joining word) and the words in the sentences need to be filled in with a preposition.

If you need a conjunction you will see (c); if you need a preposition you will see (p).

**Have a go!**

1 The cat hid (p)_________ the table (c)_________ the dog was chasing her.

2 The bird was put (p)_________ its cage (c)_________ they could get the cat out of the room.

3 My sister went (p)_________ of the door, walked (p)_________ the street, (p)_________ the road and (p)_________ the shop (c)_________ she'd said she wouldn't go.

Prepositions you might want to use:

*out under behind in up down into across over*

Conjunctions you might want to use:

*so because although as*

## Prepositions for giving directions

▶ **Fill in** the missing prepositions to tell the visitor how to get to the town centre.

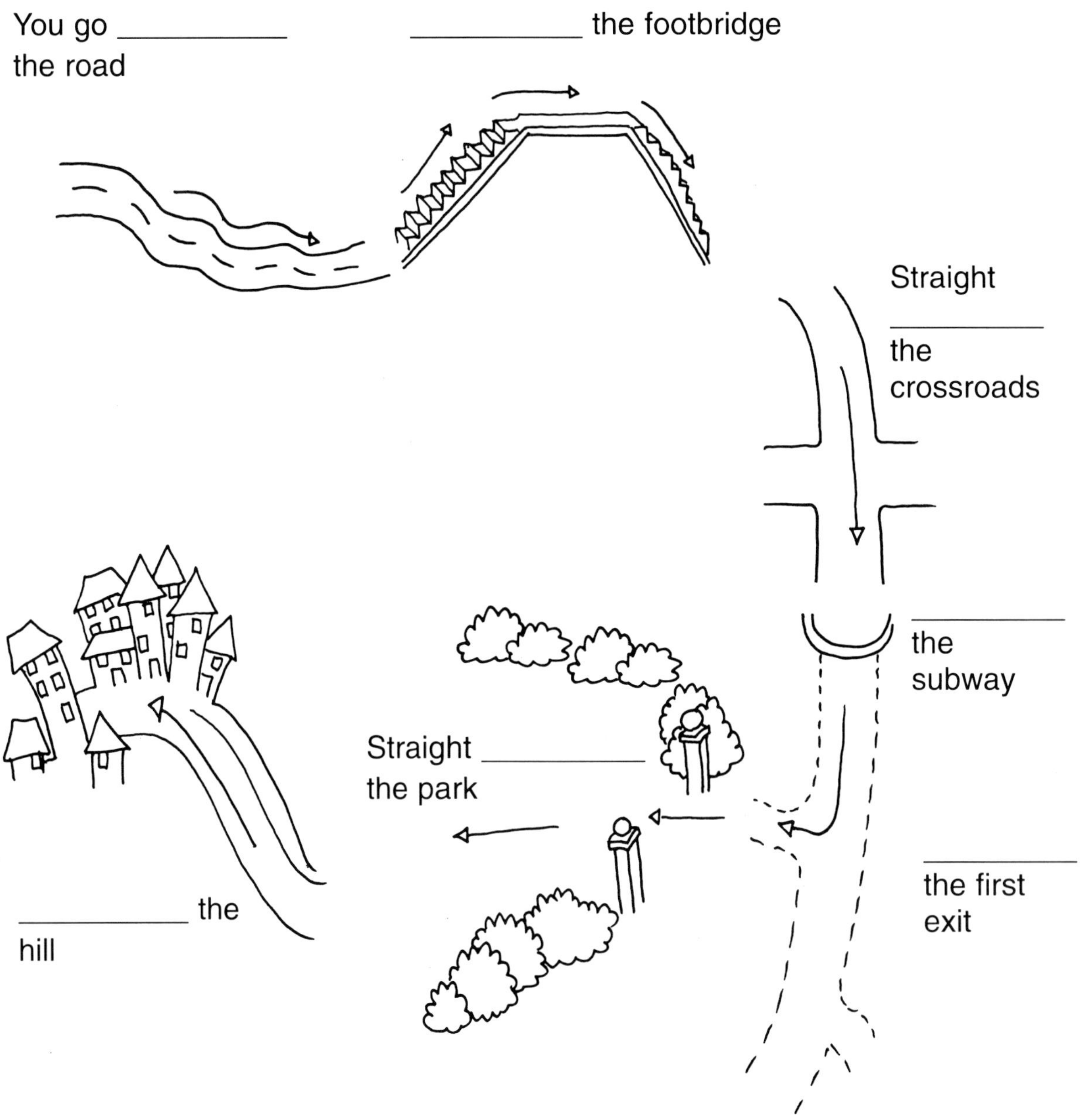

You go __________ the road

__________ the footbridge

Straight __________ the crossroads

__________ the subway

__________ the first exit

Straight __________ the park

__________ the hill

## *Order! Order!*

Just as a sentence must make sense, a group of sentences in a paragraph must also make sense.

1 **Look** at the following passage. It is taken from a book about the life of Tom Cruise, (Livewire Real Lives) but the sentences have been written down in the wrong order.

So did his dyslexia.

Tom was born in 1962.

This made learning difficult.

In his first eleven years the family moved house seven times.

He also had to move schools.

The words on the page moved as he read.

2 **Number** each sentence to put them in the correct order, so that they make sense.

3 **Read** the sentences out loud in their new order.

4 **Read** the new order to a partner. Do you both agree?

# Sequence and order

Worksheet

## *Order please!*

This is a simple map of what your day might be like.

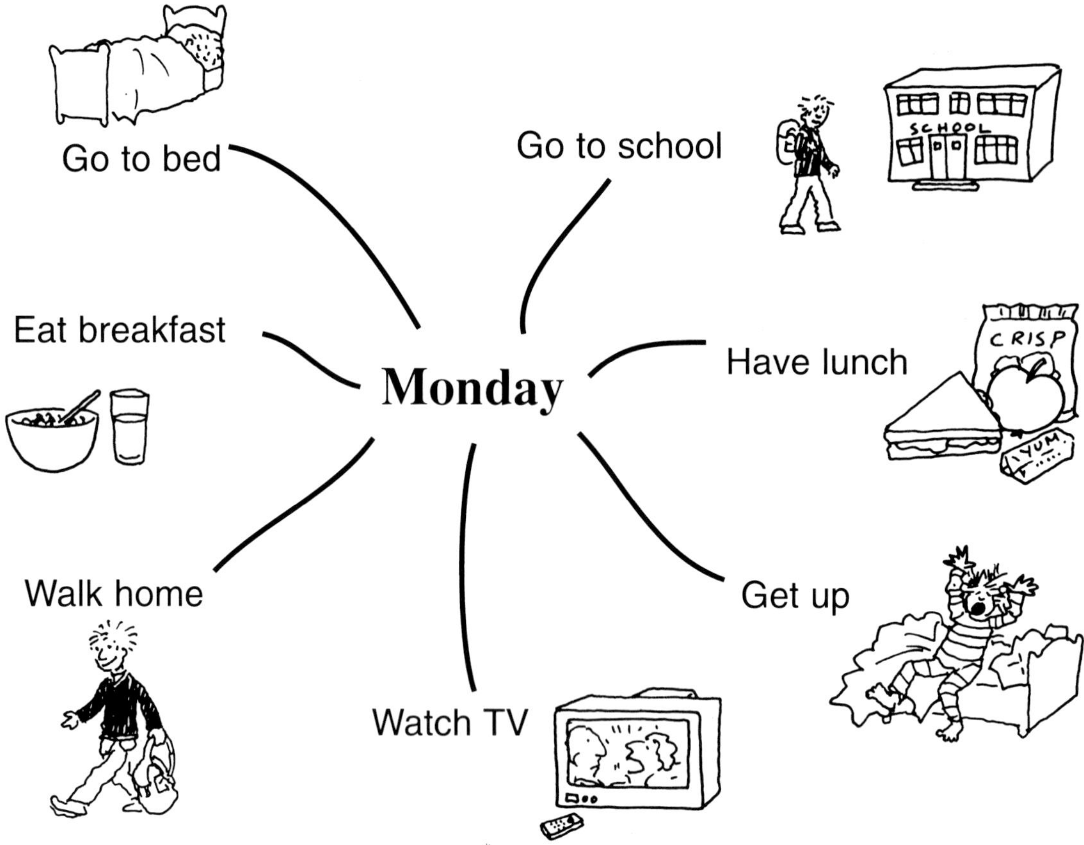


**1** Number each of the above in the order that you think they would have happened.

**2** Write out what happened on Monday, using full sentences.

Each Monday I ____________________________________________

__________________________________________________________

__________________________________________________________

__________________________________________________________

__________________________________________________________

__________________________________________________________

## *Finding the way around your day*

**1** Create a simple map of what you might do on a Saturday or a Sunday. Use pictures and/or words.

**2** Number each point in the order it happens.

**3** Write it out in sentences.

______________________________________________

______________________________________________

______________________________________________

______________________________________________

______________________________________________

______________________________________________

# Sequence and order

Worksheet

## *Logical order*

To give clear instructions, they must be in the right order.

Sally's next door neighbour asked her to feed the cats while she was on holiday. Unfortunately she left in rather a hurry, and these were the instructions she left:

There are plenty of tins of cat food.

Feed the cats twice a day.

They are in the cupboard under the sink.

The bottles of milk are in the fridge.

Let them out at the cat flap.

- **Write** the instructions out in the correct order.
- Number each one first if this helps.

1 ______________________________

2 ______________________________

3 ______________________________

4 ______________________________

5 ______________________________

# I order you!

These short paragraphs are all from the same traditional children's story, but are in the wrong order.

1 **Cut** out each paragraph.

2 Put them in the correct order.

3 **Number** each paragraph.

The furious Queen sent for her huntsman and told him to take Snow White into the forest and kill her. To prove that Snow White was dead, the huntsman had to bring back her heart in a golden box.

Once upon a time, there lived a beautiful young princess whose name was Snow White. Her stepmother, the Queen, was jealous of Snow White and treated her very badly.

Snow White wandered through the forest until she came upon a little cottage in a clearing. When she looked inside she saw it was full of cobwebs and dust. She went inside and started to clean.

The huntsman was afraid of the Queen, but he couldn't bring himself to kill Snow White. He told her to run away; then he killed a deer and put its heart into the golden box to show the Queen.

After watching Snow White in the garden one sunny afternoon, the Queen rushed to her magic mirror and said, 'Mirror, mirror on the wall, who is the fairest one of all?' She then flew into a temper when the mirror told her it was Snow White.

# Sequence and order

## *Helping to plan*

If you have a lot of writing to do, it can be difficult to organise your ideas.

Use a map to help you plan your ideas and organise your paragraphs.

This is a map that Sam drew to organise her ideas for a story she wanted to write:

5 Lady in glasses follows. Why?

1 rain
library
dust
few people

2 black hat
strange man
looking around

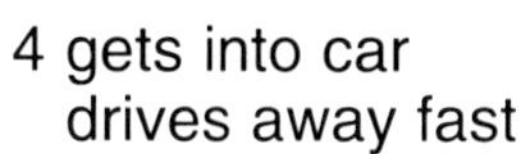

She numbered each point in the order it would come in her story.
Each point became a paragraph.
This is the first paragraph that Sam wrote:

The public library was almost empty. Outside the rain lashed against the dirty windows and the branch of a tree tapped on the glass; inside, the top shelves were dusty and untouched. The whole place had a dank, musty smell.

Choose another number from the map and write a short paragraph that you think might fit the story.

________________________________________________

________________________________________________

________________________________________________

________________________________________________

## *Ordering your own ideas*

Starting can be the most difficult part of writing.

**1** Organise your writing by using a map.

- **Choose** one of the following ideas for a piece of writing.
- **Write** it in the centre of the page.
- **Map** out all the things you might want to mention (in any order).
- **Use** pictures instead of, or as well as words on your map.
- **Number** each of the points in the order you will use it.

Ideas to choose from: *A book review; an adventure story; a letter to the council complaining that there is nothing for young people in your town; an idea of your own.*

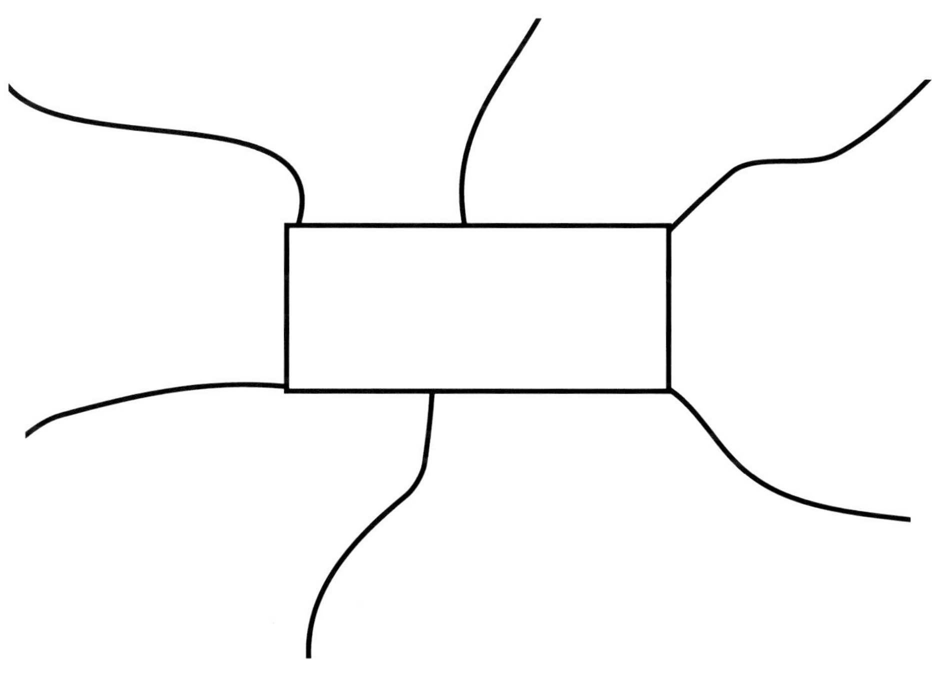

# Sequence and order

Worksheet

## *Moving on*

The following notes are taken from someone's map that they made when planning an adventure story.

**1**
Three friends holiday
Plane
Excited
Cost lots money

**2**
Take off
Pilot's voice 'Welcome to . . .' etc.
Settle down
Stewardess drinks

**3**
Bumpy
Airsick
Pilot's voice seatbelts
Stewardess worried

**4**
Strange noise
Passengers scream
Plane plunges down
Frightened

**5**
Crash landing
Burning
Debris
Bodies
Escape

1 **Choose** one of numbered sets of notes from the map. **Discuss** with a partner what you think happened.

2 **Write** the paragraph using the notes to guide you.

## *Saying it out loud and writing it down*

The words that are spoken are shown in the speech bubbles.
We can see who is speaking by looking at the pictures.

Draw a cartoon strip of your own and add speech bubbles to show what is being said.

# Written speech

## *Direct speech: What did you say?*

> Quotation marks "___" show us what somebody has said.

In writing, it is hard to tell which words somebody has said unless we use quotation marks. We usually call these *speech marks*. Quotation marks (speech marks) mark off the exact words that are spoken.

*Jim said, "Where are you going?"*
*I replied, "To catch the next train out of here."*

What did Jim say? The words that Jim said were, *"Where are you going?"*

What did I reply? I replied, *"To catch the next train out of here."*

▶ **Read** the following sentences out loud.

▶ **Highlight** the words that are actually spoken.

1 I asked Mary how old she was. She replied, "Mind your own business."

2 The shopkeeper said, "What would you like, Madam?"

3 The lady went into the store to complain. "This jacket has a mark on it!" she said.

4 Mary quoted the poem she had seen in the book,

"Roses are red
violets are blue
Most poems rhyme
This one doesn't."

## *More on speech marks*

> Speech marks are strong. They show *only* the words that have been spoken.

If you want to show the words that somebody has spoken, use quotation marks to make them stand out from the rest of your writing.

**1** Highlight the words that the person actually says in these examples.

1 Mary said, “Don’t do that!”

2 “What is the matter with you?” she asked her friend.

3 The nurse said, “How did you burn your hand?”

4 Tom asked his friend Jim a question. “Are you going to the disco on Saturday?”

5 The teacher said, “Who hasn’t done their homework?”

6 “Why did you do it?” asked the policeman.

**2** Read out loud the words that you have highlighted.

# Written speech

Worksheet

Basic Skills: Grammar and Punctuation

## *We can't stop talking*

▶ **Answer** these questions. Don't forget to add the closing speech marks.
*(Use the sentences on the last worksheet to help you.)*

1 What did Mary say?

Mary said, " ______________________________

______________________________

2 The policeman asked, " ______________________________

3 What did the teacher ask the class?

The teacher asked the class, " ______________________________

______________________________

4 The nurse wanted to know something. She asked the patient,

" ______________________________

______________________________

5 Tom wanted to know if Jim was going to the disco on Saturday. What question did Tom ask Jim?

Tom asked, " ______________________________

______________________________

# Speech marks

| The words that are spoken are kept inside the speech marks. |
|---|

*"I'm going to the shops," said John.*

The words that John **said** are, "I'm going to the shops."
John did **not** say, *said John.*

**1** Read each of the following sentences out loud.

1 "How old are you?" the shopkeeper asked.

2 James said, "My exam marks are quite good."

3 Arranging to meet his friend, Mark said, "If you get there first, put a stone on the wall. If I get there first, I'll knock it off."

- **Imagine** that you are the person speaking.
- To remember the words spoken, close your eyes, look straight across and to the left (the right if you are left handed) and **hear** the words in your head.

**2** **Write** down only the words that you would actually say if you were the person speaking. Put them in speech marks.

1 ______________________________

2 ______________________________

3 ______________________________

______________________________

# Written speech

## Deciding what is spoken

If you are not sure which words have been actually spoken, try drawing it as a simple cartoon with speech bubbles.

Jane said, “Where are you going?”

“It’s over there,” the woman directed.

▶ **Draw** the picture and speech bubbles for the sentences below on the back of your worksheet

1 “Here’s your birthday cake,” said her friend.

2 “I won!” shouted Sam as he crossed the line.

## Punctuating speech

**1** Look at the following sentences.
Highlight, or underline, the words spoken.
All the words spoken are **inside** the inverted commas.

What do you notice about the **first** word inside the inverted commas?

*"I don't really like classical music," said Jane.*

*Mary asked, "What is the name of that CD you like?"*

*"It's odd that we both like the same group," commented Sam.*

**2** Complete this sentence:
The first word that is spoken always starts with a ________ letter.

**3** Draw a circle around the capital letter of each first word spoken.

1 "Do we have to go to school today?"

2 "Why do we always get lost?" complained the man.

3 The lady said, "If you could read a map we wouldn't be here now!"

4 "This is excellent work," said the teacher.

5 "I would like two pastries," said Sue, "and two buns."

For each sentence above, you should have drawn **one** circle.

**4** Write down the first spoken word from each of the sentences.

________________ ________________

________________ ________________

________________

# Written speech

Worksheet

Basic Skills: Grammar and Punctuation

## *Carrying on the punctuation*

A comma usually divides the spoken word from the unspoken word, but it can be a question mark or an exclamation mark.

▶ **Look** at these examples:

*"Which one is it**?**" asked Sam.*
*"I am seventeen**,**" said the boy.*
*"Look out**!**" he shouted.*

**1** Write in the missing punctuation that divides the spoken word from the unspoken word. (Choose from: **, ? ! ,** )

1 "Are you coming out __ " asked Frank.
2 "I don't know what to do __ " he said.
3 "Don't do that __ " she yelled.
4 "I will be finished soon __ " replied Sam.

### Turning it around

Exactly the same rule applies. We use punctuation to separate the spoken words from the unspoken. For example:

*Sam asked**,** "Which one is it?"*
*The boy said**,** "I am seventeen."*
*He shouted**,** "Look out!"*

▶ **Write** in the missing punctuation that divides the unspoken word from the spoken. (Each one will be a comma.)

1 Frank asked __ "Are you coming out?"
2 He said __ "I don't know what to do."
3 She yelled __ "Don't do that!"
4 Sam replied __ "I'll be finished soon."

## *Splitting the sentence*

Spoken and unspoken words can be mixed together in a sentence. Punctuation helps us to see which is which.

For example:
*She is going to town said Jane but she won't be very long*

Becomes:
*"She is going to town," said Jane, "but she won't be very long."*

▶ **Read** and **check**:

The first word that is spoken is *She* so it has a capital letter.

All the words spoken are inside the inverted commas.

Commas separate the spoken parts from the unspoken parts.

(Note: If the comma comes after a word that is spoken, it goes ***inside*** the quotation marks.
If the comma comes after a word that is ***not*** spoken it goes ***outside*** the quotation marks.)

▶ In the following sentences the words spoken are in italics. **Add** the correct punctuation.

1 *I hate doing punctuation exercises* he moaned.

2 She exclaimed *I understand it*

3 *Why is it so hard* asked Peter *to get it right*

4 *All these are correct* praised the teacher

5 *These are yours* she said *and I'll take the rest*

# Tenses

Worksheet

## Tense

The tense tells us *when* something happens.

If something happens now, we use the **present tense.**
If something has already happened we use the **past tense.**
If something will happen in the time ahead, we use the **future tense.**

Today we *build* sandcastles on the beach. (Present tense)
Yesterday we *built* sandcastles on the beach. (Past tense)
Tomorrow we *will build* sandcastles on the beach. (Future tense)

**1** Each of the following sentences is given in the present tense.

- **Write** each one in the past tense and then the future tense.
- **Read** each sentence out loud.
- **Listen** carefully as you read. Have you got it right?

1 Today I make a cake.

Yesterday ______________________________

Tomorrow ______________________________

2 Maddy makes a mess.

(Past) Maddy ______________________________

(Future) Maddy ______________________________

3 I walk down the street.

Last week I ______________________________

Next week I ______________________________

## Staying in the same tense

When giving an account, do not mix tenses.

A witness was asked to give an account of an accident that had happened the day before. He tells his story in the present tense. The policeman wants it in the past tense.

"It's 9 o'clock and I walk down the road on my way to work. I'm a bit late so I need to hurry up. I cross over Silver Street, dodge between two parked cars, then out of nowhere comes this huge lorry, doing about 90 miles an hour – well OK perhaps not quite 90 but it's going pretty fast. Anyway, the driver of the lorry talks on his mobile phone, eats a sandwich and skids around the corner all at the same time. No surprise then that he goes out of control and crashes into the police car parked at the side of the road!"

▶ **Re-write** the statement for the witness, putting it into the past tense.

The first two sentences have been done for you.

"It was 9 o'clock and I walked down the road on my way to work. I was a bit late so I needed to hurry up.

_______________________________________________

_______________________________________________

_______________________________________________

_______________________________________________

_______________________________________________

_______________________________________________

_______________________________________________

# Tenses

Worksheet

## A five-year plan

**1** Think about where you want to be in five (or ten) years time.
What will you have done?
Where will you be living?
What job will you do?

This is all in the future.

**2** Fill in the gaps underneath with what you hope might happen. (See if you can come up with some really unusual ideas.)

In five years time:

I will have

______________________________

______________________________

I will be working

______________________________

______________________________

I will have got

______________________________

______________________________

In my spare time I will

______________________________

______________________________

I will also

______________________________

______________________________

## Past, present or future?

- **Look** at the statements below.
- **Connect** the statements to the 'Me' in the centre

– use a red line for the past tense
– use a blue line for the present tense
– use a yellow line for the future tense.
*(Or use another three colours if you wish.)*

I was a lovely baby.

I learned to talk very early.

I am a human being.

People say I never shut up.

**Me**

What was it like?

Maybe I'll be famous some day.

I do not like doing the washing up.

I will do it tomorrow.

The shop was shut.

I have no money.

# Tenses



## *Continuing*

A tense may also be used in a 'continuous' sense.

We say: *I sit.*
We can also say: *I am sitting.*

We may have written: *I ran.*
We may also say: *I was running.*

We can have: *I will swim.*
We can also have: *I will be swimming.*

**1** Fill in the gaps in the present tense.
*(Choose from the words underneath.)*

1 I am ________________ down the street.

2 We are ________________ to the shops.

3 He is ________________ his homework.

| doing | writing | finishing | walking | running | going | skipping |
|---|---|---|---|---|---|---|

**2** Fill in the gaps in the past tense.
*(Choose from the words underneath.)*

1 I was ________________ the dustbin.

2 They were ________________ down the hill.

3 She was ________________ on the chair.

| sitting | filling | moving | running | skiing | emptying | kneeling |
|---|---|---|---|---|---|---|

**3** Fill in the gaps in the future tense.
*(Choose from the words underneath.)*

1 You will be ________________ to school tomorrow.

2 We will be ________________ on the beach in the summer.

3 I will be ________________ you tomorrow.

| calling | going | walking | playing | running | seeing |
|---|---|---|---|---|---|

# Spot the tense

**1** Which tense have these passages been written in? Past, present or future?

▶ **Read** each passage carefully before you answer.

▶ **Check** with a partner to see if you agree.

1 It is not a good day. I know that my homework is not good and I am at risk of a detention. Why do I always get it wrong? I don't mean to mess it up, but somehow I always manage to.

Which tense? ____________

2 I am going to a brilliant concert next week. I know that not everybody will agree with me, but I know I will enjoy it.

Which tense? ____________

3 Why is it that I am wrong again? I prepare my work carefully but sometimes I just don't seem to understand what the teacher wants.

Which tense? ____________

4 I felt awful. I had promised to meet Sue outside the club at 9 o'clock, but Janie called round and I missed the bus. By the time I got there, Sue had given up waiting and gone home.

Which tense? ____________

## Getting agreement

In a sentence, the verb and the noun must agree.

In life, we all know that things are easier if we can get people to agree with each other.
It's the same in sentences. In a sentence, we must get the verb and the noun to agree with each other.
This really isn't very complicated. A singular verb and noun go together in a sentence. A plural verb and noun go together in a sentence. We say they **agree**.

**Look** at these examples:

*The dog barks loudly.*

*The dog* = the noun; *barks* = the verb.

If there is more than one dog it would be:

*The dogs bark loudly.*

*The dogs* = the noun; *bark* = the verb.

**Fill in** the gaps in the second of each of the sentences:

1 What is your name?

What __ __ __ your names?

2 I am going on holiday soon.

We __ __ __ going on holiday soon.

3 The girl walks quickly down the street.

They __ __ __ __ quickly down the street.

## Carrying on agreeing

- **Join** the sentences that have a single noun and verb with one line and the sentences that have a plural noun and verb with another line.
- Use different colours to make the two lines stand out.

The rally driver drives quickly.

The monkeys screech loudly.

The fox dives for cover.

The rally drivers drive quickly.

The monkey screeches loudly.

The policeman walks his beat.

The foxes dive for cover.

The policemen walk their beat.

# 10 Odds and ends

## The double negative

A double negative makes a positive.

Does this sound confusing?
It's really very simple.

I did something. ✓
I didn't do something.
These two sentences are quite straightforward.

But if you say: ✗
*I didn't do nothing.*
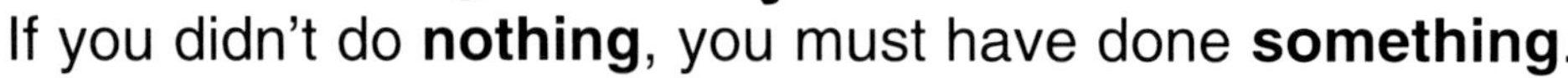
If you didn't do **nothing**, you must have done **something**.

*There was never no one there.*
'never' and 'no one' are both negatives.
So if there was *never no one* there, there must have always been someone there!

All the following sentences have double negatives.

▶ **Replace** the word in italics with a word from the box below. *(You may use a word more than once.)*

1 I can't find my homework *nowhere*.

I can't find my homework ____________.

2 Don't tell *no one* about this!

Don't tell ____________ about this!

3 I can't do *nothing* about it.

I can't do ____________ about it.

4 I didn't do *nothing.*

I didn't do ____________.

5 How dare *none* of you do nothing!

How dare ____________ of you do nothing!

| anything | any | anywhere | anyone |
|---|---|---|---|

# Making the meaning clear

Altering punctuation can change the meaning of your writing.

A class of university students was asked to punctuate this sentence:
*A woman without her man is nothing.*

The men wrote:
*A woman, without her man, is nothing.*

The women wrote:
*A woman: without her, man is nothing.*

1 These signs were seen on public roads. They have no punctuation.

Add the punctuation so that the signs clearly say what they were meant to say.

**STOP CHILDREN CROSSING**

**CHILDREN DRIVE SLOWLY**

**STOP CHILDREN**

**STEEP HILL CYCLISTS ARE ADVISED TO GET OFF AND WALK**

**FALLING ROCKS BEWARE**

**DRIVE SLOWLY MEN AT WORK**

# Odds and ends

## *I and me*

Imagine you are on your own. That will help you decide between *I* and *me*.

**1** Sometimes, it is hard to decide between *I* and *me.*

- **Look** carefully at the sentence below.
- **Read** it out loud.
- **Read** it again, leaving out the other person.

*The next door neighbours invited Dave and me to a barbecue.*

*The next door neighbours invited me to a barbecue.*

This is correct. It would sound very odd to say, 'The next door neighbours invited I to a barbecue.'

**2** Put either I or me into these sentences.
Check if you are right by leaving out the other person.

1 James and __________ went to the school play.

*(__________ went to the school play.)*

2 They asked if Julie and __________ wanted to go to town.

*(They asked if __________ wanted to go to town.)*

3 This present is for you and __________ .

*(This present is for __________.)*

4 You and __________ didn't leave the room in this mess.

*(__________ didn't leave the room in this mess.)*

5 Ruth and __________ will see to the sheep.

*(__________ will see to the sheep.)*

## *Cutting it short*

When speaking, it is usual to shorten words. These are often then written down in their shortened form.

When speaking, we often say words in their shortened form, such as:

phone – for telephone

fridge – for refrigerator

amp – for amplifier

**1** Give the commonly used shortened form of these words:

gymnasium ____________

popular *(as in pop records)* ____________

referee ____________

veterinary *(a 'doctor' for animals)* ____________

comprehensive *(as in comprehensive school)* ____________

**2** Give the full version for these words:

flu ________________

rep *(as in sales rep, or company rep)* ________________

eve ________________

telly ________________

# Practising Mapping

- **Look** at the map below.
- **What** do you think the map is about?
- **Number** each point in the right order.

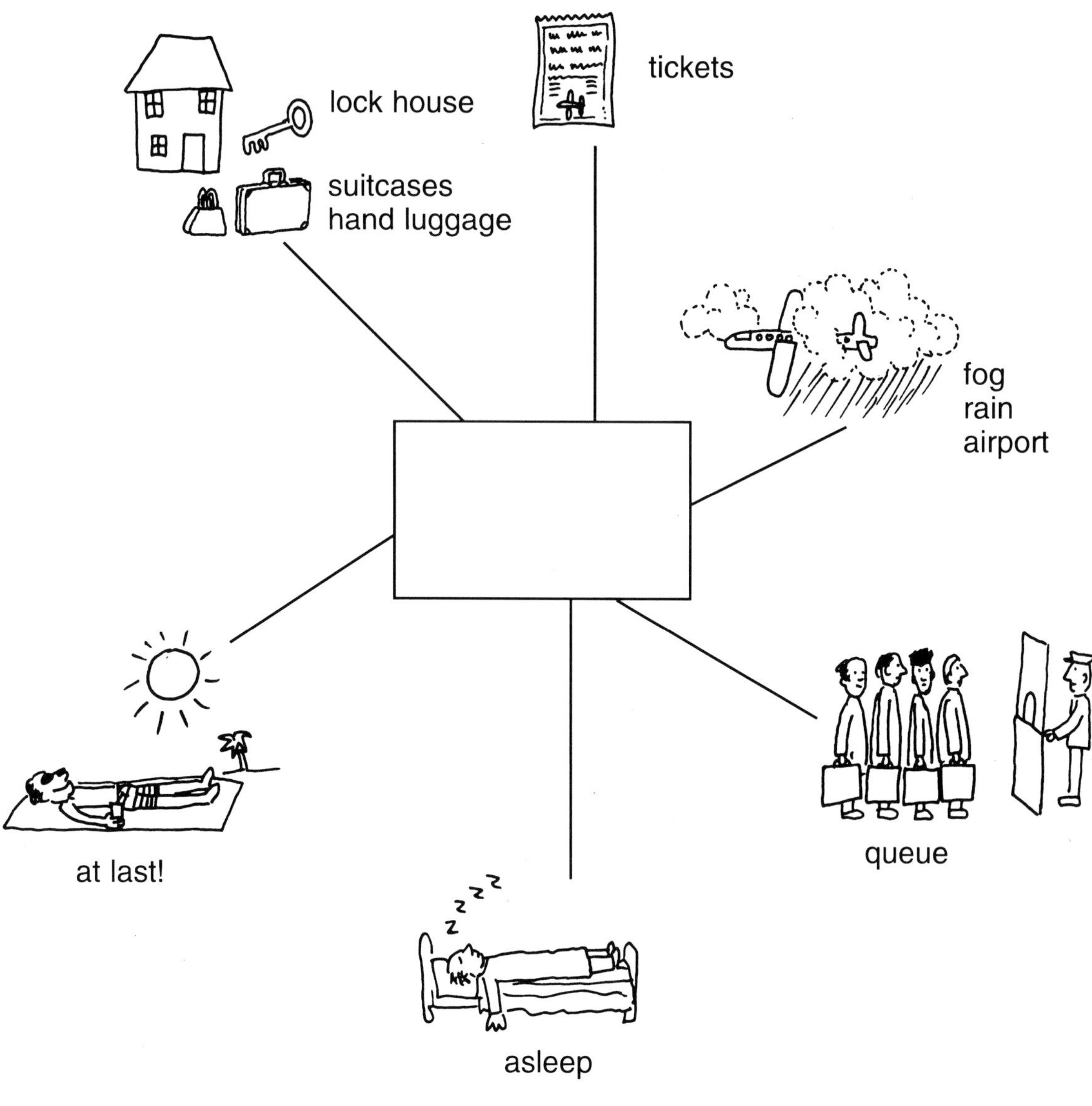

# Visual Mapping

This map is made entirely with pictures.

- **Add** some key words to the pictures to help work out what the map is about.

# 10 Odds and ends

## A jumble of errors

Strictly for fun:

- **See** how many mistakes you can spot in the paragraph below.
- **Draw** a circle around each one you can find.

matthew didnt like parties. he always felt so alone. he wasnt a mixer, like his friend charles, and nobody wanted to talk to him. What could he do to make himself more popular. I know! he thought. Ill tell them im a famous film star.
mathews friend charles thought this was a stupid idea.
What will you say when they want to know what films youve been in? he asked.
matthew didnt care. It was either telling them he was a film star or telling them hed won the lottery – but then they might want to borrow money, so no, a film star it would have to be

- **Check** your answers against the correct version below:

Matthew didn't like parties. He always felt so alone. He wasn't a mixer, like his friend Charles, and nobody wanted to talk to him. What could he do to make himself more popular?
"I know!" he thought. "I'll tell them I'm a famous film star."
Matthew's friend Charles thought this was a stupid idea.
"What will you say when they want to know what films you've been in?" he asked.
Matthew didn't care. It was either telling them he was a film star or telling them he'd won the lottery – but then they might want to borrow money, so no, a film star it would have to be.